Original title:
How to Find Meaning in a Netflix Marathon

Copyright © 2025 Creative Arts Management OÜ
All rights reserved.

Author: Dean Whitmore
ISBN HARDBACK: 978-1-80566-069-9
ISBN PAPERBACK: 978-1-80566-364-5

Portraits of Life Behind the Screen

In the glow of flickering light,
Couch cushions are my throne tonight.
Popcorn dreams, I munch and sip,
Reality fades, I take a trip.

Netflix gods, with choices vast,
Binge-watching spells me, I'm outclassed.
In a world of plot twists and schemes,
I search for meaning in my memes.

Characters laugh, have epic fights,
They teach me lessons on cozy nights.
Whispers and screams, the drama unfolds,
While I critique in my comfy folds.

If I lived in their shoes, would I thrive?
In my soft PJs, I'm broken but alive.
So here's to tales both silly and grand,
From my couch, I rule this vast cinema land.

Emotions Untangled Through the Screen

Binge-watching is my cardio,
Couch-potato champion, you know.
Characters cry, and I just laugh,
Plot twists serve like a warm bath.

Popcorn flies, the dog on my lap,
Lost in worlds that feel like a trap.
Who knew that aliens had such taste?
Guess my brain's now taking a break!

Stories Written in Silence

Silent moments filled with glee,
As I watch a cat chase a bee.
No need for words, my heart beats loud,
In quirky plots, I feel so proud.

Laughing hard 'til my sides ache,
Zooming through tales like getting a shake.
Who knew despair could be so fun?
A twist in the tale, and I'm on the run!

Connections Beyond the Credits

We laugh, we cry, in glorious spree,
Cinematic madness, just you and me.
Friendships blossom with every show,
In this universe, we let our minds flow.

Characters come, and then they depart,
Yet they leave a mark deep in my heart.
Sharing memes while the credits roll,
Life's just a series, start to console!

Shimmers of Insight in a Series Finale

Final episode, attention on peak,
With theories drawn, we passionately speak.
Shimmers of wisdom in lines once bold,
Yet here I sit—with popcorn uncontrolled!

The screen fades black; then we all sigh,
What's next? Twinkies? A quick pie?
As reality hits, I laugh at the mess,
In this ridiculous quest, I feel so blessed!

The Intermission of Self-Discovery

In pajamas, I ponder my fate,
With snacks piled high, the fridge is my mate.
Each cliffhanger reveals some insight,
Between episodes, I laugh and I fright.

As credits roll, my wisdom grows,
In binge-watching, a strange truth glows.
The couch is my throne, snacks are my food,
I swear, someday, I'll alter my mood.

Reflections on the Couch of Life

Remote in hand, I search for the gold,
In stories of love, adventure, and bold.
I mirror their struggles and silly plight,
My own life looks better in dim, soft light.

In monologues, I find wisdom profound,
Between chuckles, new revelations abound.
Each episode's flavor, a dish served in fun,
On this endless sofa, my soul's gently spun.

Vignettes of Existence in Every Episode

Each plot twist like life's little pranks,
Surprises unfold—give thanks, give thanks!
Between sips of soda, my lessons do flow,
Like heroes on screen, I too will grow.

From awkward dates to the villainous jeer,
I find in the fiction a familiar cheer.
Vignettes of existence, I mimic and tease,
In the wild world of binge, I'm utterly at ease.

Lessons Learned from Ensemble Casts

With every season, my wisdom expands,
An ensemble of quirks, a life unplanned.
Each character's failure brings laughter and tears,
In the drama of life, I confront all my fears.

Like them, I misstep, I stumble, I trip,
Yet rise with more jokes, a comedic script.
Together we navigate love's playful dance,
Embracing the chaos with each crazy chance.

The Art of Lost Hours

Binge-watching, time dissolves,
What day is it? Who cares at all!
Snack wrappers pile like trophies won,
As plot twists unveil, and we just have fun.

Lost in worlds beyond our own,
Mundane thoughts have gently flown.
With every click, the saga grows,
A secret life, the couch allows.

Characters Who Speak in Silence

Eyes meet eyes, no words are said,
Yet heartstrings pull, we're both well-read.
Facial expressions, endless chats,
In mute dramas, we're the aristocrats.

With every glance, a tale unfolds,
More gold than silver, truth be told.
Forget the dialogue, watch their grace,
In silence found, we find our place.

Unboxing Life Inside the Stream

Each episode, a gift to unwrap,
Like birthday boxes, they fit in a lap.
Plot lines twist like a curly fry,
With each reveal, we laugh or cry.

Characters live in digital frames,
Yet somehow, we remember their names.
Remote in hand, like a magic wand,
We dive into dreams, and swiftly respond.

Finding Within the Fragments of Fiction

Lost pieces of life we try to gain,
In scripted tales, our truths remain.
Relatable woes from characters bold,
Their laughter and tears, pure treasure untold.

With every scene, we stitch our thoughts,
In vivid pixels, happiness taught.
Between the laughs, the cries, and sighs,
We find ourselves in their goodbyes.

The Essence of Life in Every Scene

In a sofa kingdom, I reign supreme,
Chasing plot twists like a wacky dream.
Lost in characters who laugh and cry,
I find my wisdom as the snacks run dry.

A couch potato sage, so wise, so grand,
Balancing chips and popcorn in hand.
Life lessons served in two-hour bites,
Who knew truth could hide in Netflix nights?

Romantic comedies, thrillers, and more,
Each genre opens a metaphoric door.
With laughter and joy, my spirit ignites,
Each movie a gem, lighting up my nights.

From the couch, the world feels far away,
Yet I'm traveling far with each binge today.
So here's to the tales that make us giddy,
In streaming we find the meaning, how witty!

Threads of Humanity Through Fiction

In a series of laughs, humanity's shown,
With quirks and oddities, I'm never alone.
Characters teach me the quirks of their lives,
As I munch on snacks, the story thrives.

From quirky pilots to detectives with flair,
Each episode offers a little despair.
Yet in their struggles, I find my own,
These fictional folks feel like homegrown.

When aliens land, or robots chat loud,
I ponder existence, feeling quite proud.
A high-speed chase or an awkward date,
Reminds me that life's just a twist of fate.

So I laugh, I cry, in my binge-watching spree,
Each saga unfurling a part of me.
Finding compassion in pixelated dreams,
Their tales are as rich as life's funny themes.

Discoveries Along the Streaming Path

Click, click, binge, as the hours fly by,
Learning more from the screen than I thought I'd try.
Each character's blunder, a lesson so bright,
Turns my lazy evening into philosophical insight.

Scrolling through options, what genre to choose?
An epic adventure, or a tale of blues?
Finding meaning in chaos and love's sweet embrace,
The stories unravel, a humorous race.

With every cliffhanger, my heart skips a beat,
Wondering if the hero will savor defeat.
Yeah, life is a puzzle, with pieces galore,
Netflix and wisdom, who could ask for more?

So I settle down, snacks piled high,
Winking at fate through the screen's gleeful eye.
In this streaming wonder, I laugh and I dream,
Each episode ends, but the memories gleam.

Glimpses of Truth in Fictional Realms

Fiction spins tales that tickle my mind,
Where characters dance, leaving sanity behind.
A witty remark or a plot that surprises,
Life's tangled answers in humorous guises.

With each twist and turn, I shuffle along,
The absurdities dance, an illogical song.
Monsters and heroes, lost in their quest,
Reminding me gently, I'm truly blessed.

In the realm of the screen, life's lessons unfold,
In laughter and chaos, the universe told.
A villain becomes just a friend on the run,
In fictional worlds, we find joy and fun.

So here's to the platforms of laughter and light,
Illuminating truths in humorous sight.
I escape through the pixels, my heart's on flight,
In streaming realities, everything feels right.

Temporal Drift in the Binge-Wave

On the couch, I take my seat,
Snack in hand, world feels complete.
Episodes blur, time slips away,
My life's on pause, I'm here to stay.

I've seen a dog speak Spanish now,
And a bright unicorn with a cow.
Plot twists twist like pretzels, oh dear,
Did I really just binge three seasons here?

Friends text, 'Hey, are you alive?'
I respond, 'Just living the five.'
Life outside can wait a bit,
For massive plots that truly fit.

The fridge is empty, but who cares?
I've got my laughs and quirky stares.
In every episode, I find my cheer,
Each joke sharper than a spear!

A Symphony in Cinematic Moments

Press play, the lights dimmed low,
My popcorn's dancing, what a show!
Characters sing like Broadway stars,
All while I lounge beneath the bars.

Rom-coms leave me swooning loud,
Making me wish for a crowd.
Dramas come with twists galore,
While I chuckle, 'Please, just one more!'

The interludes cause snacks to fall,
I laugh so hard, I barely sprawl.
These moments make my heart do flips,
Even when the plot tightens its grips.

As credits roll, what have I gained?
Connections made, the joy unchained.
In this theater between walls,
I've found myself in countless halls!

Through the Window of the Digital Realm

Click, click, a portal swings wide,
Inside this world, come for the ride.
Characters navigate this verse,
While I binge on laughs, it's just a curse!

Every cliffhanger leads to snacks,
And when I stand, I hear my back cracks.
How many hours have slipped away?
Lost in tales and crazy play.

Voices echo from fictional lands,
As I gesticulate with my hands.
They can't hear me, but that's just fine,
I'll critique plots with a glass of wine.

Like moths to the glow of screens afire,
We lose control, but who's to tire?
In laughter's embrace, I may take flight,
In this digital realm, the world feels right!

The Comfort of Unseen Companions

Beside me, ghosts of favorites cling,
With each punchline, they joyfully sing.
Companions made of pixels and dreams,
My heart dances, or so it seems.

The TV hums a soothing tune,
With each episode, I'll be immune.
Their trials become my own delight,
As I chuckle deep into the night.

Every plot twist, every cheer,
Brings me warmth, almost like beer.
In this glow, loneliness flies away,
For in this world, I choose to stay.

And when the credits start to roll,
I realize they've touched my soul.
These unseen friends made me believe,
In laughter, love, we can achieve!

Resilience in the Stories We Tell

Binge-watched heroes, capes in their hands,
Rescue the world with lazy demands.
Sagas unfold, so much to unearth,
Procrastination? Oh, it's a marathon of mirth!

Popcorn mountains, a fortress we build,
As plots thicken, yet time feels distilled.
With every episode, we round the bend,
In showbiz, our fears come to mend!

Epic love tales, and villains so sly,
What's the moral? Don't forget to reply!
When life dares to knock, we shout, "Not today!"
In the world of streaming, we always play!

A couch potato's dream, laughter ignites,
Through twists and turns, we reach dizzying heights.
From drama to comedy, we take a stand,
Resilience grows in this whimsical land!

Connecting Threads in Fiction's Fabric

Characters lost in a streaming haze,
We search for wisdom in a million ways.
In fitting stories, truth weaves its thread,
While laundry piles high, in fiction we tread.

Plot twists aplenty, surprises galore,
Is the hero real, or just a folklore?
Lost loves and laughs in a cosmic dance,
In the middle of it all, can we find a chance?

Mysteries solved with a cup of joe,
As epic battles rage on the screen,
Exploring the depths, we giggle and sigh,
In the realm of make-believe, we learn to fly!

Barreling through stories, our hearts feel light,
In fiction's embrace, we're free from fright.
Bonding through tales, we share a sigh,
Connecting the dots, oh my, oh my!

Hidden Lessons Beneath the Credits

As credits roll, we gather round,
Lessons in laughter, wisdom abound.
Who knew a sitcom could reveal the truth?
In snappy one-liners, we find our youth.

With each new show, a mirror we see,
Reflections of life's absurdity.
In cozy blankets, we laugh and we cry,
Peeking through dramas, we learn to fly.

Behind every hero lies a tale untold,
Of struggle and joy, of being bold.
In finales, we twirl, embracing the jest,
For every good binge, we've learned from the best!

So here's to the credits, the lessons they keep,
In the world of stories, we dive in deep.
From sitcoms to thrillers, we binge with glee,
Hidden lessons emerge as we watch with glee!

The Veil of Reality and Make-Believe

Soft blankets wrap us like a warm embrace,
In fiction's art, we find our place.
Reality fades, plotlines engage,
With every episode, we turn the page.

Between the laughs, we ponder and sigh,
In dramatic scenes, we often reply.
Do we live in dreams or in tales we weave?
When the show ends, it's hard to believe.

A world crafted clear, yet chaotic and wild,
We jump through the screen, like a curious child.
With quirky characters and wild intent,
In this realm of make-believe, we find content!

So as we settle for another long night,
Let's dive in deep, chase the next delight.
In the clouds of humor and heart's reprieve,
Reality's veil is ours to conceive!

Building Bridges Through Fictional Worlds

On the couch we gather, snacks in hand,
Lost in stories from a distant land.
Heroes and villains clash in fright,
While we ponder life, half through the night.

Mysterious plots keep us glued and tight,
Adventures unfold, what a curious sight.
Between each episode, laughter and tears,
A bond forms strong, banishing fears.

Characters teach us with each wild plot twist,
In their strange worlds, reality's missed.
We cheer for the wins, we cringe at each fail,
A shared escapade, we set our sails.

So here we sit, popcorn in our lap,
Reaching out with joy, breaking the map.
In cinematic realms, we gleefully roam,
Finding our meaning in this quirky home.

The Language of Emotion in Film

Silent screams beneath the bright glow,
We laugh at the jokes, let the feelings flow.
Each frown and grin, a universal tongue,
In every scene, a new song is sung.

Romantic woes or a friend's sweet chat,
We dive deep into emotion, imagine that!
With every frame, we mirror our plight,
As the hero stumbles, we hold on tight.

Tears fall freely over popcorn snacks,
While we dissect love, hear the heart's cracks.
With a dramatic gasp and an awkward dance,
We find in each story a funny romance.

So let's hit rewind, savor each line,
In a world of laughter, our hearts intertwine.
Navigating feels on a whimsical ride,
Finding our truth with our favorite guide.

Artefacts of Existence in Series

In each episode, a treasure we seek,
Finding wisdom hiding, though plotlines are bleak.
Who knew a sitcom could spark such a thought?
The quirks of our lives, in chaos we're caught.

Characters mirror our own wild spree,
With their faults and joys, we're all family.
The closing credits roll, but the laughter stays,
As we ponder our lives in a hilarious haze.

Each plot device, a lesson well-drawn,
In worlds so absurd, our sorrows are gone.
From hilarious quotes to heartfelt goodbyes,
We gather the fragments, our spirits on high.

So here's to the screen, our enchanting guide,
Through ridiculous tales, we joyfully slide.
Letting each moment turn into a cheer,
Finding life's meaning, binge-watching with beer.

Poetic Moments in Cinematic Time

Lights dim down low, the show begins bright,
In a whirl of colors, we take flight.
Laughing at love and flubbing the lines,
Each frame a poem, where laughter defines.

With each plot twist, we're caught in the thrill,
Time pauses gently, our hearts get a chill.
Tears may trickle or giggles would soar,
These fleeting moments, who could ask for more?

As characters bumble through lives they can't plan,
We find the humor in each crazy jam.
In the middle of chaos, we find our bliss,
In the realm of the silly, we steal a kiss.

So let's celebrate, with joy in our hearts,
Through cosmic chuckles, each soul imparts.
In the magic of film, we bravely unwind,
Finding our laughter, in stories aligned.

Melodies of Meaning Amidst the Credits

A snack in hand, my eyes do glaze,
As credits roll in a dazzling haze.
I ponder life, as plots unwind,
What wisdom lies in what I find?

The sofa's my throne, the remote, my scepter,
In binge-watching bliss, I search for a vector.
Each episode's gems swirl in my mind,
Hope this is deeper than popcorn combined!

The characters laugh, cry, and shout,
Teaching me lessons without a doubt.
In the silly moments, truths slither near,
Like finding deep meaning in a squirrel's cheer.

So here's to the stories, both wacky and wise,
In my living room couch world, I reach for the skies.
With laughter and tears, I connect through this art,
In marathon journeys, I find a new start!

Embracing Chaos in Every Plot Twist

At first glance, all seems so mundane,
Just another series, predictable strain.
But wait! A twist - the hero's a cat?
Now that's the kind of chaos where I'm at!

I dive into plots like a whimsical sea,
Confused by the characters as they jive freely.
The villain's a grandma who knits on a spree,
What meaning is wrapped in this comedy?

As seasons unfold, I ponder the lesson,
In fights over snacks, I find my confession.
Sometimes, the chaos breeds laughter and glee,
Is my life a sitcom? Well, wait and see!

With each new twist, my heart starts to race,
Embracing the madness, I find my own place.
Through giggles and gasps, I gather my wits,
In a world of chaos, the humor fits!

Revelations in the Closing Scene

The finale approaches, tension fills the air,
Will the duo unite or fall into despair?
With snacks as my sidekick and cozy attire,
I'm poised for the truth, like a detective in fire.

The credits roll, and I laugh out loud,
What a wild ride! I'm lost in the crowd.
Was the meaning there, hidden in the jest?
Or did I just binge what I loved the best?

As the screen fades, my mind starts to muse,
Each binge-worthy story gave me some clues.
In dialogue snappy, and plots gone awry,
I find my reflections that make me sigh.

So here's to the stories that make us awake,
In sleepy moments, new paths we shall take.
Finding meaning in twists, laughter's delight,
What can I say? These shows feel so right!

Finding Myself in the Flickering Lights

Flickering lights paint stories so bright,
Each frame a chance to ponder the night.
On the couch I sit, snacks scattered wide,
As I search for that meaning just beneath the tide.

Characters scream, and the jokes do fly,
Like a squirrel with sass, I laugh and cry.
Finding solace in stories that make hearts align,
Is wisdom waiting there, or just punchlines divine?

As plotlines tangle like shoelaces lost,
I find myself giggling, ignoring the cost.
What's real and what's fiction? Who's counting the hours?
Amidst in the chaos, I'm sprouting fresh flowers.

So here's to the laughter, the tears, and the fun,
In a marathon journey, we're all on the run.
Through the flickering lights, my spirit takes flight,
In these crazy tales, I embrace the delight!

Journeys Through Pixelated Dreams

In the glow of screens we dive,
Lost in plots that seem alive.
Characters laugh, cry, and scream,
As we float in a pixelated dream.

Popcorn bowls like mountains grow,
With each episode, our moods flow.
Reality fades, who needs a plan?
We journey through films, hand in hand.

Binging tales till dawn breaks,
Relationship woes? That's why we take,
A seat on this couch, hearts feel light,
As we chuckle in our cozy night.

Through laughter shared and tears we cry,
Finding purpose, oh my!
In every line and funny scene,
Life's sweet meaning feels like a dream.

The Heartbeat of an Endless Episode

The intro jingle plays so sweet,
Another binge, what a treat!
With snacks piled high, we take a seat,
The heartbeat thumps to a digital beat.

We plot twist, pause, and rewind,
In this world, treasures we find.
Yet as credits roll, we're left bemused,
What day is it? We're rather confused.

Waiting for the next great thrill,
Our fridge is empty, but who needs a meal?
For laughter shared and cries that leak,
These endless episodes leave us unique.

So here we sit, in joy or strife,
Searching for meaning in this TV life.
For as the saga continues to grow,
We're all just friends, don't you know?

Threads of Emotion Through Cinema

A sofa fortress, cozy and wide,
We conquer tales, side by side.
In each emotion, we laugh and sigh,
As the credits roll, we wonder why.

Tangled in dreams as stories unfold,
Heartfelt journeys, both warm and bold.
With every twist, we huddle near,
Ridiculous romances and villainous sneers.

Our hearts race fast, our bellies ache,
Binge-watching fits, oh, what a mistake!
But let it roll, no use for a clock,
In this realm, the fun's in the shock.

So here we are, caught in frames,
Drawing laughter from the wildest games.
In this world of fiction's embrace,
We find our meaning, at our own pace.

Flickering Thoughts Between Scenes

Flickering lights, we laugh and cheer,
The plots twist, yet we persevere.
With every pause, our snacks decimate,
Wondering if we've gained or lost weight.

As actors scheme and dance around,
In these moments, meaning is found.
Laughter spills like popcorn air,
Craziness here, not a single care.

Transfixed by stories, absurd and grand,
Chasing dreams, hand-in-hand.
We giggle and gasp, in sync we rise,
With every twist, our spirits surprise.

In a labyrinth of episodes divine,
Every giggle, every whine.
Flickering thoughts between the streams,
Life's humorous truths weave through our dreams.

Endless Scrolls of Solitude

In a world of endless choices,
I scout for joy in unclear voices.
Cartoon cats chase coffee cups,
While my brain remotely erupts.

Seasons blend in a dizzying haze,
Finales leave me in a daze.
Was that romance or an alien plot?
Guess I'll never know, but it sure was hot!

The fridge hums a lonely refrain,
Leftovers stare with disdain.
Yet, I chuckle at the droll scenes,
Laughing at life from plush machine.

As the credits roll down the screen,
I'm trapped in a laugh of my own routine.
With every click, a story's told,
In this cozy chaos, I find my gold.

The Quest in Quantum Flicks

A quest begins on couch-bound lands,
With popcorn mountains in both hands.
Paranormal dramas, oh what a thrill!
What time is it? Oh dear, I'm late for my meal!

Characters jump through the virtual air,
With plot twists hidden everywhere.
Wait, how did they get there from here?
Did I just laugh or shed a tear?

A knight in shining armor's plight,
Turned out to be a wizard's bite.
Rabbits popping, wise men squawk,
In the land of binge, the clock's just talk.

So here I sit, eyes wide as skies,
Lost in stories that never die.
With every episode, a giggle greets,
In quantum flicks, my boredom retreats.

Echoes of the Binge-Watcher

In the silence of my living room,
Characters gather, forging doom.
Evil laughs from my glowing screen,
As I munch on chips, my snack cuisine.

I cheer for heroes, cry for the foes,
Why do I even care how this goes?
Twists so wild, I beg for more,
Each episode, an open door.

Sinking deeper in tales untold,
Is this wisdom? Or just bold?
The echoes of laughter bounce off the walls,
As I chase each plot twist, my mind enthralls.

In a fluff of chaos, I find my bliss,
Giggling at whimsy, how could I miss?
For every cliffhanger, a snack awaits,
In this binge, my spirit radiates.

Illuminated by the Screen's Glow

Bathed in light from my trusty screen,
Each flick reveals where I've never been.
From dragons to space, it's quite the spree,
As I giggle and gasp, just me and me.

Characters throw shade like a sunny day,
Their banter is gold, come what may.
Plotlines twist like a pretzel knot,
I laugh, I sigh, Oh boy, what a lot!

The fridge calls, but I'm on a roll,
A caffeinated buzz makes me feel whole.
With every scene, my worries disappear,
In this illuminated world, magic is near.

As the last credits begin to scroll,
I dance with joy, feel it in my soul.
In screens and laughter, life's sweet blend,
This marathon of fun, may it never end!

Seeking Truth in Animated Worlds

In cartoons where cats chase their tails,
Wisdom hides in the craziest trails.
With each plot twist, we laugh 'til we cry,
Yet wonder, can we also just fly?

A dragon that hiccups throws fire in fun,
Who knew that with laughter, we'd outshine the sun?
So let's binge on these antics, it's pure escapism,
Laughing is better than existentialism!

Parallel Journeys Wrapped in Laughter

Two best friends on wild escapades,
Finding humor in every charade.
With snack-filled nights and silly plots,
We bond over jokes and forget our lots.

In parallel worlds, we're kings, we're queens,
Chasing laughs in our fluffy routines.
Plot armor makes us invincible, sure,
As long as the popcorn's always in store!

Reflections on Pause: Pondering Plotlines

When the screen freezes, our minds start to whirl,
Does the hero eat snacks or just save the world?
Picture-perfect romances, they bloom on cue,
But can they binge like we do?

Characters pause with a theatrical flair,
And we muse on their tales while lounging in chairs.
In this world of jest, we seek for what's right,
In dreams of adventure, we laugh through the night.

Chronicles of Comfort in Carousel View

Press play on the chaos, the laughter takes flight,
In stories that spin like a carousel night.
Each character winks, pulls us in,
As we snuggle up close and let the fun begin.

In binges of brilliance, we polish our quirks,
Unraveling plots that drive other folks berserk.
With a cup full of comfort and laughs like a breeze,
These tales teach us joy as we snack and tease.

Frames of Contemplation

Binge a series, snacks in hand,
Lost in tales that stretch so grand.
Philosophers muse in comfy chairs,
While pants are optional—who even cares?

Plot twists twist my brain in knots,
Characters' lives are more than thoughts.
A universe unfolds with every click,
As time escapes, our minds it pricks.

What's a dream? What's a plot fake?
Didn't I have plans? Oh, what a mistake!
When did life steer clear of its lanes?
I'll figure it out when the next season reigns.

Witty remarks fill each episode,
While I ponder my own little code.
In between the laughs and tears,
I find my meaning—a snack, it appears.

Echoes in a Screen's Glow

In the glow of my screen, I waste away,
What's real is lost in the dramatic play.
Fictional friends have more fun than I,
But I cheer them on, my spirit is high!

Adventures span across the couch,
While my laundry continues to slouch.
Are they my pals? Or just pixels in line?
Either way, they all drink my wine!

As episodes blend into one long dream,
Life seems funnier than it would seem.
Why do chores when laughter awaits?
I'll organize my heart—oh yeah, it can wait!

In between banter, I seek some sense,
My thoughts wander off, all tense and dense.
Is there wisdom in this endless spree?
Yes, for tomorrow, I'll finally watch TV!

The Art of Pause in the Stream

The magic button, pause in the fray,
Gives me a moment to contemplate play.
Do I dare to resume this epic plight?
Or spend ten more minutes crafting my bite?

Episodes stack like a lean-to of tales,
Overflowing popcorn—a mountain that fails.
With each story, I laugh, maybe cry,
Life's complexities wrapped up in a fry.

The keen art of snacking, they show with finesse,
While existential dread offers a mess.
Is this art or just Netflix-designed?
Creative block, my mind feels blind!

Yet in the chaos, solace I find,
In quirky lines made bizarrely aligned.
I pause, reflect, then hit "next" in delight—
Finding meaning—even inside the night!

Sagas of Solitude

In shadows I sit with a bowl full of chips,
As heroes and villains engage in fierce quips.
Solitary moments, oh, what a treat!
With cushions for company, I can't feel my feet!

In the saga of solitude, laughter unfolds,
A thousand adventures, in memory I hold.
Why face the world when the screen's such a glow?
I'm living my best life—don't you know?

Between a melodrama and a cliffhanger crush,
I reckon my dreams while munching at rush.
Who needs the sun when the glow brings fun?
In this world of pixels, my fears are outrun!

As credits roll and my eyelids droop,
I snuggle deeper into this cinematic loop.
Like the characters, I plot my next quest,
A checked-out soul, but in binge, I rest!

Flickering Narratives of Bedtime

In the glow of the screen, I'm lost,
Plot twists are cheap, but I'm the cost.
Pajama-clad dreams, my popcorn throne,
Binge-watching chaos, my mind overblown.

The dog needs a walk, but who has the time?
Superheroes leap while I ponder my rhyme.
Snack crumbs like stars scatter across my lap,
I seal my fate in this couch-warm trap.

With each episode, I find a new quest,
A villain, a hero, who could guess the rest?
Flirting with fate through the capes and the foes,
I laugh at the drama; it's nobody's woes.

The clock strikes five, but I'm still in place,
Chasing down stories in a caffeinated race.
Sleep's just a rumor; adventure's my plight,
As the flickering narratives fade into night.

Reels of Reflection: A Couchside Diary

Sipping cold coffee, I snack on regrets,
Plot holes like black holes, no logic begets.
Scrolling through titles, like fishing for gold,
A thousand new tales in the brave, remote hold.

My cats throw their paws as I dive down the lore,
Each twist a delight, yet I crave something more.
Are they just actors? Or mirrors of me?
We laugh, we cry—what a life—on the TV!

With plots like a whirlwind, I navigate time,
A couchside philosopher, sifting each rhyme.
My heart races fast as romance unfolds,
Yet a dance with reality grimly holds.

The credits roll down, I'm left in a daze,
Did I learn a lesson, or just lost in a haze?
As I wipe the last chip crumbs from the screen's glare,
I'll ponder it all while I refuel my chair.

Stories Unspooled in Darkened Rooms

In velvet darkness, my kingdom resides,
The stories unspool as I munch and abide.
Dim lights flicker tales of glory and strife,
Characters dance in this digital life.

A pirate, a dragon, a robot named Lou,
Plot lines stretch thinner than my patience too.
Each cliffhanger ending, my heart skips a beat,
Navigating plot twists while tripping on feet.

As scenes dazzle brightly, my eyes start to droop,
Silent screams echo, I'm lost in the loop.
Why resolve anything when I have dessert?
I'd rather unwind than look up from my shirt.

So bring on the drama, the laughs, and tears,
In binge-worthy moments, I'll suppress my fears.
With popcorn explosions, I play my sly game,
In this wild, wild world, nothing's quite the same.

Navigating Dreams Between Episodes

The sofa's my ship, the remote's my steer,
Sailing through genres fueled by snacks near.
Each season like waves in a tempestuous sea,
I board different vessels—what will I be?

A lawyer, a detective, or just a bright cat?
I'm someone else for a while, and that's that.
Laughs bubble up with a chuckle or two,
Couchmates in secret, my very own crew.

Yet when credits roll, like the sun with a sigh,
Reality whispers, "Hey! You must try!"
But wait, one more episode, just one little taste,
Adventures await; let's not go to waste.

So here I shall linger, in laughs and in thrills,
My thesaurus of dreams feeds my mind with more fills.
With each laugh and each cry, I'm wildly alive,
Navigating life on this couch I will thrive.

A Quest for Connection in the Stream

Binge-watching tales, a cozy delight,
Characters bond, chasing day into night.
Who's the hero, who's the fool?
I relate too much, am I losing my cool?

Couch companions sharing popcorn and fate,
Marathon sessions, oh what a state!
A love for shows, and pizza slice one,
We laugh as the credits obscure the sun.

Friends in the screen, they see me awake,
Can they tell I'm just one big mistake?
With plot twists and jokes, we all relate,
Our hearts synced with drama, oh what a fate!

So here's to the magic of streaming's embrace,
Where I find my meaning in a warm, fuzzy space.
Laughter and tears, all wrapped in a reel,
Connection through stories, that's just how I feel.

The Mirror of My Soul in Cinema

On the sofa I sit sporting mismatched socks,
Watching folks dance, as my phone gently mocks.
Is that me on screen? Darn, I'm a cliché!
In this wild world, I'm just here to play.

Rom-com antics fuel my deep yearning,
While villains plot, I'm inwardly turning.
Who needs a therapist when Netflix is free?
The drama unfolds, and so do I, you see?

Reflections abound in this flickering light,
I laugh at their pain while I sip my Sprite.
Each episode's a lesson, wrapped in a joke,
Here's my mirror, and it's barely broke!

So let's dive deep into this cinematic flow,
Finding pieces of me in each high and low.
With popcorn in hand, I embrace the bizarre,
For each flick on the screen, I'm a shining star!

Uncovered Insights Between the Frames

As I hit play on another grand quest,
I settle in, it's prime-time zest.
Lost in the laughter, the drama spins tight,
A scholar of nonsense on a cushy flight.

One-liners and quirks, they spark much thought,
Who knew this binge-watching gave so much plot?
The wisdom of elders wrapped up in jest,
Turns couch-surfing into life's little test.

Lessons are learned in the silliest tales,
Why does the villain get such fine gales?
Between the laughs, a nugget or two,
I ponder my life and what's really true.

So here's to the frames that bridge the divide,
Finding depth where I thought I'd just hide.
For each playful moment, I'm feeling blessed,
In this chaotic rhythm, I finally rest.

Dreams Validated in Laugh Tracks

With laughter aplenty, the screen lights up well,
I cheer for the failings of sitcoms I'll tell.
Every punchline lands, like a soft, friendly hug,
Cringe-worthy moments make the heart tug.

In scripted chaos, my dreams find a way,
Characters falling face-first every day.
Shouting at screens, my pals understand,
Together we laugh, as we munch on the brand.

The wicked plots twist with joy and surprise,
Life's too darn short, so here's to the cries!
Validation sparked by a snicker or two,
Finding my worth in a laugh I pursue.

So let's sing along with the canned applause,
To the silliness and warmth that inevitably draws.
In this world of screens, I find my own light,
With dreams validated in humor's great flight.

Dialogues That Define Us

On the couch we sit, Netflix ablaze,
Characters chat in their quirky ways.
We laugh and we cry, in a binge-fueled spree,
Breaking news: I've decided I'm a star on TV.

Popcorn is flying, what's next on the list?
An epic romance or a monster twist?
While scrolling and giggling through plot turns so grand,
I'll end up more confused than I ever planned.

The thrill of the chase as the series unfolds,
Every cliffhanger boldly, my heart now sold.
In cheesy dialogues, truths sneakily glint,
Who knew my soulmate was a guy with a tint?

And here's to the drama we can't take away,
As life imitates art, in a comical way.
So pass me the remote, let the saga continue,
In this crazy ride, oh how I feel so in tune!

The Narrative of Our Lives in Streaming

Binge-watching dreams in my fuzzy PJs,
Plot explosions happening in quirky ways.
The serial kisses, the sci-fi battles galore,
A hero emerges, who could ask for more?

With each episode, we're glued to the screen,
Finding our worth in the laughs and the scene.
In shadows and dramas, reflections may rise,
Did I just hear a truth or a really bad lie?

In sitcoms that tell me to lighten my load,
I ponder deep questions on a snack-filled road.
Is this progression or character cram?
I'll tell you after one more episode, oh man!

So stream on, dear friends, let the stories ensue,
In pixelated realms where nothing is new.
We search for the meaning over snacks we confide,
In universe-expanding tales that we can't set aside.

Cinematic Escapism and Self

Lost in the world of a film's wild ride,
Dreaming of chicken wings, and popcorn piled high.
Where villains are silly, and heroes are bold,
I find my truest self in these stories retold.

A rom-com heart that skips beats with delight,
While ghosts in the plot jump out, fear in the night.
My identity now, a montage on replay,
A love for the absurd, in this dramatic foray!

Do I relate to a cat or a band of misfits?
In laughter, I find wisdom, and in fails, pure hits.
With plot strands connecting my life and my soul,
It's hard to explain but it feels like my goal.

So here's to the stories that make us feel whole,
In the warmth of the flicks, we regain our control.
With laughter as balm, and a plot twist or two,
In cinematic bliss, we rediscover the new.

Flickering Images and Forgotten Dreams

In the glow of the TV, past dreams get a spark,
My couch is the ship through the love and the dark.
With each sassy quip and the laugh track I hear,
I find joy in the chaos—oh dear, what a year!

The dazzling stories, the twists that bemuse,
Living through pixels while I snooze and I snooze.
Through art I find meaning, a comedy jam,
And suddenly, I feel just as grand as a glam.

With flickering frames, I explore who I am,
From dragons to dating, all wrapped in a plan.
In every wild plot, in each over-the-top,
I tap dance my way to a Netflix soft stop.

Dear binge-watchers, unite in our fate,
In this slightly absurd, cuddly, Netflix state.
We may not have answers, but we have a good laugh,
As we race through our series, and forge our own path!

The Hidden Treasures of a Screen

On the couch, I dive so deep,
In search for laughs, or maybe sleep.
Each episode, a brand-new quest,
Can this sitcom really be the best?

With snacks piled high, my fortress strong,
Binge-watching feels so very wrong.
But wait, is that a plot twist there?
I gasp and spill my soda—oh, despair!

Characters bloom, they laugh and cry,
I bond with strangers, oh my, oh my!
Solving mysteries while I snack,
Who needs a life when I've got this track?

So here I sit, with no regrets,
Each season-end, I feel the sweats.
With popcorn bowls and hearts aglow,
I chase each treasure, on this screen, we go!

Evolution Through Entertaining Episodes

From cavemen drawn to drama's arts,
We've come so far, we've made a start.
With laughs and tears, the stories flow,
Who knew evolution would zig-zag so?

In cozy sweats, I hit play again,
Discovering the lives of my couch-bound friends.
From heroes great to villains flawed,
I cheer them on while feeling awed.

A sitcom here, a thriller there,
All struggles blend in my comfy lair.
From plot arcs wild to wacky schemes,
The real world fades, it's just a dream.

With every scroll, my heart ignites,
Learning lessons from the digital lights.
I laugh, I snort, and sometimes sigh,
Evolution's truth? It's just one more try!

Rewind, Reconsider, Repeat

Click, rewind, what did I miss?
Was that a joke or just sheer bliss?
A frantic search, my heart on fire,
For hidden gems, I just can't tire.

Friends bicker over next week's lore,
I nod along, but I want more!
"Let's watch that episode for the sixth time,"
We laugh and argue, it feels sublime.

Power naps between those plots,
"Wait, who's that? I've frankly forgot."
Moments blend into one big mess,
But I embrace it, I couldn't care less.

As seasons shift, I hit replay,
Struggles fade in comedic ballet.
Life's mysteries in pixelated art,
Rewind, reconsider—let's not depart!

Fragments of Life in the Rearview

The couch, my world, my rearview wide,
Collecting fragments, with arms open wide.
From love stories that make me sigh,
To plots so silly, I just can't lie.

I see my past in every scene,
Like a quirky dream where I've been keen.
I laugh at moments misplaced in time,
Enjoying this madness—a perfect crime.

Characters shine, they ebb and flow,
Teaching lessons I didn't know.
From famished dragons to superheroes cool,
Oh, how I do love this endless school!

So here's to fragments, let's cherish each hour,
Amidst the giggles, I feel the power.
With every click, I piece together,
Life's joyful puzzle—will last forever.

Sifting Through Netflix's Multi-Colored Lens

Click, click, scroll, a frenzy ensues,
Colors flash — what on earth to choose?
Action, romance, or a true crime spree?
Decisions, decisions! Oh, why is this me?

Diving deep into a sea of bad clips,
Laughing hard at the plot with odd flips.
Realizing halfway, I've clicked the wrong show,
But now I'm stuck, I guess it's a no-go!

Each thumbnail a siren, it beckons with flair,
'Watch me!' it calls, like a Netflix snare.
With snacks in my lap, I commit to the ride,
Who knew I'd be laughing while feeling inside?

A binge-worthy sprawl on the couch feels just right,
As absurdities blend into a glorious night.
Tomorrow's regrets are tomorrow's sad fate,
But tonight? I'm a hero in myth and in fate!

The Lullaby of Entangled Plots

In a world of confusion, plots twist and turn,
A hero, a villain? Or am I just burned?
Lost in the layers of a storyline thick,
I chuckle and cringe at each curveball they pick.

Oh, dear characters, you drive me quite mad,
With backstories wild, how could they be sad?
Mismatched romances while chaos breaks through,
A love for the silly, oh yes, that's my view!

They're saving the world but forget the local cat,
Staring in shock — now where's the humor at?
Their lives are more hectic than mine on a Tuesday,
Yet still I'm squinting—what's next in this crazay?

As credits roll in, I stand up and laugh,
Understanding nothing but loving the craft.
In tangled storylines, there's clarity found,
Each giggle a hint that joy can abound!

Connections Made in Streaming Shadows

In dim-lit rooms, we gather to stream,
A virtual party, or so it may seem.
Between snacks and laughter, connection is real,
Who knew that a sitcom could help us all heal?

Remote in one hand and popcorn in tow,
With twists in the plot, we laugh till we glow.
The bonds that we build in between every scene,
Turn strangers to friends, blood, laughter, and green.

Yet, mysteries linger—what's even the goal?
Finding deep meaning in comedic droll roll.
When logic escapes, and the humor takes flight,
We find common threads in the silliness bright.

So here's to the binge, the laughter, the fun,
The quirky connections that can't be outrun.
In streaming shadows, our hearts intertwine,
Finding joy in the madness? That feels just divine!

Seeking Clarity in Character Arcs

Oh character arcs, you twist and you bend,
One moment a hero, the next, you're a friend.
With backstories tangled, you dance through each show,
I laugh till I cry, through each ebb, each flow.

Dramas unfold with a laugh or a tear,
Why take it all seriously? Come on, we cheer!
When plots get too heavy, we just raise a toast,
To the characters that we love—oh, we love them the most!

In absurd escapades, they lead me along,
Encouraging laughter, they hum their own song.
So here's to the tropes, the clichés, and the jokes,
Through arcs that confound, we outsmart all the hoaxes!

As credits run wild, I smile with delight,
In character chaos, I find pure insight.
Life's a wild ride, like that binge-watching spree,
Finding joy in the antics, just let yourself be!

Echoes of Laughter in the Dark

In the glow of the screen, we sit tight,
With snacks piled high, it feels just right.
Characters flicker, they laugh and they cry,
We guffaw and we gasp, oh my, oh my!

Couch potato kings, we wear our crowns,
In this kingdom of binge, we never frown.
Fast forward the plot, rewind all the fun,
Clearly, the night is just getting begun!

With popcorn in hand, we cheer for the chase,
Each plot twist brings smiles to this cozy space.
We high-five the screen for the best one-liners,
Comedic gold found in all the designers!

Yet deep in our hearts, there's something quite strange,
These fictional lives seem close, yet so far away.
Yet here we are, snug, in our blanket cocoon,
In this echoing laughter, we make our own tune.

Intimacy Found in a Screen's Glow

The lights dim down, we share a laugh,
With every scene change, we craft our own path.
In this embrace of pixels and glee,
The romance is odd, but it sets us free!

Dialogue dances, and hearts start to race,
In this electric bubble, we find our place.
We root for the couples, we yell at the foes,
This quirky world is where friendship grows.

No dinner or date, just chips by the bowl,
From bad puns to plots that can take quite a toll.
Still we gather 'round, favorite shows up ahead,
Forgetting our worries, our stress simply fled.

So here's to the nights wrapped in laughter and cheers,
In this cuddly chaos, we forget all our fears.
As the credits roll down, we might shed a tear,
But deep in our hearts, we know love's still near.

Constellations of Stories Across the Universe

Galaxy of plot lines, oh what a delight!
We travel through realms, from morning to night.
Cosmic absurdities, they're our guiding stars,
In the multiverse of giggles, there are no bars.

Aliens, wizards, or fools in disguise,
Each episode brings us to new highs and lows.
We map the constellations of laughter and fear,
Discover heroism in characters dear.

With mindless bliss, we journey afar,
On this sofa spaceship, you're my shining star.
Through mysteries tangled, and plot holes galore,
We embrace the sweet chaos, always wanting more!

So here's to our travels through fantastical lands,
Hand in hand, with popcorn and unforgettable plans.
We'll explore every season, together we'll soar,
In this infinity of laughter, who could ask for more?

Heartfelt Layers Beneath the Surface

Beneath flashy faces and laughs on the screen,
Lies a world of emotion, and it's quite unseen.
We giggle at tropes, but there's more to explore,
With layers of humor that leave us wanting more.

We root for the underdogs, we cheer for the brave,
Finding wisdom in silliness, our hearts they do save.
In the comfort of couches, we find our own truth,
The hilarity mixing with echoes of youth.

Each dramatic moment wrapped in a jest,
Unraveling stories that put us to the test.
We laugh at our passions, as we sip and snack,
In this heartfelt realm, we've got each other's back.

So together we dive into antics and dreams,
Navigating plots with our shared silly schemes.
In the marathon glow, we seek and we find,
A connection, a chuckle, uniquely entwined.

Whispers of Wisdom in Dialogue

In the flicker of the screen's embrace,
Lifelong truths hide in every face.
Glimpses of wisdom, as plotlines twist,
Like eating chips, I can't resist.

Characters teach with every quip,
Yet I snack on comfort from the chip.
Conversations deep, or just absurd,
Can be quite profound, or just plain weird.

Couch-bound guru of the binge-watching spree,
Finding life lessons 'tween cups of tea.
Arguments over whose turn is next,
They sharpen my wits, are far from vexed.

Escape to the Illumination of the Screen

A glow at midnight pulls me near,
In the cozy warmth, I shed my fear.
With popcorn ready, and drinks in tow,
I seek my escape, just sit back and glow.

Every plot twist is a wild ride,
I laugh and cry, then roll with pride.
Life's a puzzle, and I'm just a piece,
In a world where chaos finds its peace.

Adventures await in each uncanny tale,
Where dragons roar and heroes prevail.
And though it's just fiction on the screen,
These stories breathe life — or so it seems.

Searching for Truth in Storylines

Digging for gems in plot and jest,
Between seconds, I get life's test.
Visions of love, betrayal and plight,
Help me reflect on my own night.

I ponder characters, their flops and fails,
In their turmoil, my heart exhales.
Searching for truths in every show,
Gems of wisdom hidden, like snow.

I laugh at the foolish, I root for the bold,
Concerned for the floundering, and the enfold.
Every click of 'next episode' rings true,
Life lessons emerge in episode two.

Navigating Life Between Seasons

Between the seasons, I take a break,
Filling my heart with joy, no mistake.
When a cliffhanger leaves me on edge,
I wave my remote, ready to hedge.

In the gaps of plot twists and charms,
I find my life's meaning, a world without harms.
A world where laughter bends time's scope,
And every giggle fills me with hope.

As credits roll and sadness fades,
I lock in my favorite character parades.
In chasing each season, I learn to unwind,
The silly, sweet moments my mind can find.

Fragments of Humanity Behind the Screen

Binge-watching strangers feels just right,
In pixelated lives, we find delight.
We laugh, we cry, from our cozy seat,
As characters gather for a virtual meet.

Popcorn spills like secrets untold,
Remote in hand, we become so bold.
From drama to comedy, we misbehave,
Knowing our hearts, the screen might save.

For every plot twist, there's a sigh or cheer,
As fictional friends draw us near.
Reality fades, just us and them,
Lost in the flicker of a lighted gem.

So let's toast to tales, both strange and grand,
In the glow of the screen, we make our stand.
With every episode, we uncover more,
Humanity shines through each opened door.

Dreamt Narratives in the Glow of Midnight

At the stroke of twelve, we dive in deep,
Worlds collide as we lose sleep.
Fictional warriors wielding their swords,
We're couch-bound heroes with epic hoards.

Oh, the plot twists that bend our minds,
In this midnight haze, true wisdom finds.
With each cliffhanger, our laughter roars,
As reality waits outside our doors.

We morph into villains or star-crossed love,
In cozy blankets, we rise above.
As characters dance through our dreams and schemes,
A marathon journey with laughter in beams.

Sipping tea, we ponder the quest for gold,
Stories unravel as nights unfold.
In this world of pixels, we seek the light,
In every funny moment, our hearts take flight.

The Soul's Whisper in Streaming Shadows

With every episode, we learn and live,
The wisdom of scripts begins to give.
Through laughter and tears, we share the plight,
Streaming shadows dance in the night.

With each passing scene, our thoughts entwine,
Bonding with characters, we sip on wine.
A quirky plot twist, a dash of flair,
Unlock the secrets we choose to share.

To the intro's tune, we nod our heads,
In our comfy pajamas, we're blissfully led.
As stories collide like waves on the shore,
In this strange land, we find folklore.

So let's embrace the tales that we weave,
In streaming shadows, there's magic to believe.
With humor wrapped tightly in every frame,
In this wild marathon, we're never the same.

Moments of Clarity Amidst Chaos

In chaos of scenes, a pattern appears,
As we munch on chips and sip on beers.
From the couch, we reign over the land,
Inspecting life with a remote in hand.

Each episode mocks our daily grind,
As we laugh out loud, leaving stress behind.
The subtle jabs at our hushed despair,
In jestful banter, we find our flare.

Beneath the humor, there's truth laid bare,
As quirky characters give us a dare.
To find the humor in what we face,
This chaotic world becomes our space.

So here's to the laughter, the lessons learned,
In moments of clarity, where joy's returned.
With every replay, dreams resound,
In this Netflix realm, true treasures abound.

www.ingramcontent.com/pod-product-compliance
Lightning Source LLC
Chambersburg PA
CBHW070748220426
43209CB00083B/193